Learning Catalan on the Go
An Introduction for Beginners

by

David S. Luton

Copyright © David S. Luton 2017

ISBN:978-1977869760

Table of Contents
1. Introduction – 5
2. Pronunciation – 7
3. The Verbs *tenir* (have) and *necessitar* (need) – 13
4. Definite and Indefinite Articles – 14
5. In Class – 17
6. School Subjects – 19
7. Greetings, and Useful Phrases – 20
8. People and Introductions – 27
9. The Family – 33
10. Professions – 36
11. Countries, Cities and Languages – 40
12. Clothes and Colors – 48
13. The Body – 53
14. Days, Months and Seasons – 56
15. Numbers and Dates – 59
16. Telling Time – 64
17. Activities – 67
18. The Verb *anar* (to go) and Places – 71
19. Asking for Directions – 75
20. Talking about the Weather – 79
21. The Home – 71
22. Animals and Nature – 84
23. Food and Drink – 88
24. Basic Grammar – 97
25. Adjectives – 113

26. Describing People and Things – 117
27. Forming the Plural – 121
28. **Apprendix**: Around Town in Valencia – 129

Introduction

The Catalan group of languages including *mallorquí* (the form of Catalan spoken in the Balearic Islands) are the closest languages to the Occitan language spoken in parts of southern France (including the traditional *provençal* language of the famous *troubadours*!). Apparently, the speaking of Catalan is more widespread in the region of Catalonia (including the city of Barcelona) due in part to a political and cultural influence and pressure which promotes a "Catalan only" mentality. In the Valencian Community, on the other hand, Spanish is much more widely spoken, especially in the larger cities, and Valencian is more widely spoken in the villages (in some cases exclusively) outside of the large cities. Even in large cities like Valencia, there are a significant number of native speakers of the Valencian language who use it at home, even if not in public.

Places Where the Catalan group of languages are spoken:

1. The Catalonian region of Spain (including Barcelona)

2. The Valencian Community in Spain

3. The Balearic Islands in Spain (Majorca, Menorca, Ibiza)

4. Small parts of the Aragón and Murcia regions of Spain

5. Roussillon and Perpignan in southern France

6. The nation of Andorra

7. The city of L'Alguer in the Italian island of Sardinia

La pronunciació

The **Vowel Sounds** in Catalan are not as simple as those in Spanish since many have long and short or open and closed sounds. I will try to simplify it in this way:

a – like *father*, or somewhere between *father* and *cat*; when unstressed sometimes like /ə/

e – like *café* or *get*, but when unstressed sometimes like /ə/, esp. in at the end of a word, e.g. *sempre* (always)

i – usually as in the word *police*

o – like *go* or somewhere between *go* and *hot*, also like *oo* as in *food*, especially in an unstressed syllable

u – like *rude* or perhaps sometimes shorter

Diphthongs

Theoretically, the diphthongs in Catalan should be the same as Spanish, but I've found that sometimes they merely represent the first vowel sound. For example:

ai – as in the German work *Kaiser*, but sometimes more like the a of *father*
(vaig – I go, faig – I do)

oi – like *oi* in the word *toilet*, but sometimes more like the *o* of the word *go* (*boig* – crazy)

au – normally like ow as in the word cow (like au of sauerkraut)

ei – like *ei* of the word *freight*

Consonants

ç – like s, the same as in French and Portuguese

g – like *go* when followed by *a, o* or *u* and like *gel* when followed by e or i

-ig – at the end of a word like *sh*
boig – crazy
faig – I do
vaig – I go
veig – I see
roig - red

h – always silent, e.g. *hola*

j – like j in English, not like a Spanish j

l – sometimes almost nasalized at the end of a word, but you can always pronounce it like a normal l and that will be fine

ll – usually like y in yes, the same as in Spanish

l·l – like ll in English

qu – like in English when followed by a or o; like k when followed by e or i

r – rolled when double or beginning a word, the same as in Spanish, a *final r* is often *silent*

s – like an s, but like a z when occurring between vowels

t – sometimes *silent* at the end of a word, e.g. *molt bé, anar fent*

tx – like *ch* in the word *church* (e.g. *cotxe*)

x – **Normally** like *sh* (e.g. *xicot*), **occasionally** like x in English (e.g. *taxi*), or in some cases like *gs* or even *s*

Accent and Stress

The easiest rule to remember is that you will always stress the syllable where you see a written accent mark. For example:

anglès
València
països

If there is no written accent mark, you will normally stress the last syllable of words ending in a consonant other than s, and the second to last syllable of words ending in a vowel or the consonant s. For example:

bo**nic** (ends with a consonant other than s)
bo**ni**ca (ends with a vowel)
bo**ni**ques (ends with the consonant s)

With words ending in –ia, you will normally stress the vowel i and pronounce it as a separate syllable if the word contains no written accent. For words where this *i* is not stressed, you will normally see a written accent mark over a different vowel and the i forms a dipthong with the vowel *a* that follows (i.e. -ia are pronounced as one syllable). Please note, that words that normally have an accented i in Spanish, won't have an accent in Catalan or Valencian, although the i is still stressed. For example:

carnisseria (final i *is* stressed, this would be *carnicería* in Spanish)

València (final i is *not* stressed because of the accent mark over the e)

A l'aula
(in the classroom)

tenir - to have

jo **tinc** – I have
tu **tens** – you have (familiar)
vostè **té** – you have (formal)
ell/ella **té** – he/she has

nosaltres **tenim** – we have
vosaltres **teniu** – you all have
ells/elles **tenen** – they have

Tinc un llibre. – I have a book.
No tinc un llibre. – I don't have a book.

Expressions with the Verb *tenir*

tenir **calor** – to be hot
tenir **fam**/tenir **gana** – to be hungry
tenir **fred** – to be cold
tenir **ganes** – to feel like (doing something)
tenir **por** – to be afraid
tenir **pressa** – to be in a hurry
tenir **set** – to be thirsty
tenir **son** – to be sleepy
tenir **sort** – to be lucky
tenir **vergonya** – to be ashamed

necessitar – to need

jo **necessito** – I need

tu **necessites** – you need (familiar)
vostè **necessita** – you need (formal)

ell **necessita** – he/she needs
ella **necessita** – he/she needs

nosaltres **necessitem** – we need

vosaltres **necessiteu** – you all need
vostès **necessiten** – you need (formal)

ells/elles **necessiten** – they need

Necessito el llibre. – I need the book.
No necessito el llibre. – I don't need the book.

un – a/an (masculine)
una – a/an (feminine)

uns – some/a few (masculine)
unes – some/a few (feminine)

un llibre – a book
uns llibres – some books

una goma – an eraser/rubber
unes gomes – some erasers

el, l' – the (m. singular)*
la, l' – the (f. singular)*

els – the (m. plural)
les – the (f. plural)

el llibre – the book
els llibres – the books

la classe – the class
les classes – the classes

*You will use **l'** before most singular nouns beginning with a vowel or an h, regardless of gender (there are some exceptions like *la història* and *la universitat*).

Subject pronouns in Catalan: *jo* (I), *tu* (you), *ell* (he), *ella* (she), *nosaltres* (we), *vosaltres* (you all), *ells* (they-m.), *elles* (they-f.) – are optional, that is to say that it is not necessary to use them when not needed for emphasis or clarity. To simplify things, I will often omit the formal pronouns *vostè* and *vostès* which do not have separate verb forms, but rather use the same forms as *ell/ella* and *ells/elles* respectively.

L'aula
(the classroom)

Tinc... – I have...
Necessito... – I need...
Veig... – I see...
Vull... – I want...

l'**alumne** – the pupil/student (m.)
el **bolígraf** – the pen (or *el boli*)
el **capítol** – the chapter
el **company** – friend, co-worker, mate (m.)
el **curs** – the course
l'**escriptori** – the desk
l'**estoig per a llapis** – pencil case
l'**estudiant** – the student (both genders)
el **llapis** – the pencil
el **llibre** – the book
el **mestre/professor** – the teacher (m.)
l'**ordinador** – the computer
el **paper** – (the) paper
el full de paper – the sheet/piece of paper
el **paràgraf** – the paragraph
el **pupitre** – the student desk
el **quadern** – the notebook
el **retolador** – the marker
el **tema** – the theme, topic, subject
els **apunts** - notes
prendre apunts – to take notes
els **deures** - homework

l'**aula** – the classroom
l'**alumna** – the pupil/student (f.)
la **cadira** – the chair
la **classe** – the class
la **cola** – the glue, paste
la **companya** – the friend, co-worker, mate (f.)
la **frase** – the phrase, sentence
la **impressora** – the printer
la **lletra** – the letter
la **llibreta** – the notebook
la **lliçó** – the lesson
la **goma** (d'esborrar) – the rubber (eraser)
la **grapadora** – the stapler
la **maquineta** – the pencil sharpener
la **mestra/professora** – the teacher (f.)
la **motxilla** – bookbag, backpack, rucksack
l'**oració** – the sentence
la **pàgina** – the page
la **pantalla** – the screen
(e.g. computer screen, movie screen)
la **paraula** – the word
la **pissarra** – the board, blackboard
la **taula** – the table
les **tisores** – the scissors

Les assignatures escolars
(school subjects)

Jo estudio... – I study/I'm studying...
Nosaltres estudiem... – We study/We're studying...

Jo aprenc... – I learn/I'm learning...
Nosaltres aprenem... – We learn/We're learning...

l'**àlgebra** – algebra
l'**anglès** – English
el **castellà** – Spanish
el **català** – Catalan

la **biologia** – biology
la **ciència** – science
l'**educació física** – physical education
la **geografía** – geography
la **història** – history
la **informàtica** – IT/computer class
la **llengua castellana** – Spanish literature
la **llengua catalana** – Catalan literature
la **química** – chemistry
les **arts plàstiques** – art
les **ciències naturals** – natural science
les **matemàtiques** – math(s)

Greetings and Farewells

Les salutacions (greetings)
Bon dia. – Good morning.
Bona tarda. – Good afternoon.
Bona nit. – Good evening.
Hola. – Hello./Hi.
Digui! – Hello! (answering the phone)
Ei! - Hi!/Hey! (informal)

Com estàs? – How are you? (familiar)
Com està (vostè)? – How are you? (formal)*
Com esteu? – How are you all? (familiar)
Com estan (vostès)? – How are you all? (formal)*
Com va això? – How's it going?
Com va tot? – How's everything going?**

*You should use the formal with strangers or in formal or business-like situations, especially when speaking to superiors or people who are older than you. You can use the familiar with friends and family members, people younger than you who are not superiors and even people who are older than you if they are relatives or family members.

***tot* (all/everything); *tots* (all/everyone); *tothom* (*everyone*)

Les respostes (responses)
jo *estic*... – I am...
tu *estàs*... – you are... (familiar)
vostè *està*... – you are... (formal)
ell *està*... – he is...
ella *està*... – she is...

nosaltres *estem*... – we are...
vosaltres *esteu*... – you all are... (familiar)
vostès *estan*... – you all are... (formal)
ells/elles *estan*... – they are...

bé – fine/well
molt bé – very well
malament – bad/not well
no molt bé – not very well
terrible – terrible
anar fent – okay, so-so

Bé, i tu? – Fine, and you? (familiar)
Bé, i vostè? – Fine, and you? (formal)
Bé, i vosaltres? – Fine, and you all? (familiar)
Bé, i vostès? – Fine, and you all? (formal)
Ho sento./Em sap greu. – I'm sorry.
Ho sento molt. – I'm very sorry.

Els adéus/comiats (farewells)
Adéu. – Good-bye./Bye.
Bona nit. – Good night..
Fins després./Fins ara. – See you later.
Fins demà. – See you tomorrow.
Fins aviat. – See you soon.
Me'n vaig. – I'm going now./I'm leaving.
Que vagi bé! – Take care./All the best!
Ens veurem./Ens veiem. – See you around.

Les paraules/frases útils
(useful words and phrases)

sí – yes
no – no
potser – maybe, perhaps
És clar! – Of course!

Em sembla que... – It seems to me that...
Crec que... – I believe that...
Per cert... – By the way....

A veure… - Let's see…

senyor- sir/Mr.
senyora – ma'am/Mrs.
senyoreta- miss/Miss

o sigui... – that is to say.../in other words...
doncs – well, then, so then

Oi? – Is that so?
Exacte./Exactement. – Exactly.
Perfecte! – Perfect!
D'acord. – Okay. (Agreed.)

Ostres!/Òndia! – Gosh!/Gee!/Wow!
Quina sorpresa! – What a surprise!
Ui! – Oh!/Oh my!/Oops!

Genial! – Great!
Apa!/Vinga va! – Come on!/Let's go!
Vinga! – Come on!*

Si us plau. – Please. (formal)
Sisplau. – Please. (informal)
Perdó. – Sorry! (e.g. when bumping into someone...)
Disculpa. – Excuse me.
(e.g. to ask a question - familar)
Disculpi. – Excuse me. (formal)
Ho sento./Em sap greu. – I'm sorry.
(I feel bad)

Gràcies. – Thank you./Thanks.

Moltes gràcies. – Thank you very much.
De res. – You're welcome.
Benvingut!/Benvinguda!
Benvinguts!/Benvingudes! – Welcome!*

Un brindis! – I propose a toast!
Salut!/Xin-xin! – Cheers!
Salut! – Bless you! (after a sneeze)
Bona sort! – Good luck!
Bon profit! – Bon appetit!
Una abraçada! – A hug!/Hugs!
Felicitacions!/Enhorabona! – Congratulations!

Ho sé. – I know.
No ho sé. – I don't know.

Ho entenc./Ho comprenc. – I understand.
No ho entenc. – I don't understand.

Què és això? – What is this/that?
Què vol dir això? – What does this/that mean?

*These are the forms that correspond to masculine singular, feminine singular, masculine plural and feminine plural, respectively. Please see the section on adjectives.

Pot...? – Can you...? (formal)
Pots...? – Can you...? (familiar)

Pot parlar més a poc a poc, si us plau?
Can you please speak more slowly?

Parli més a poc a poc, si us plau.
Please, speak more slowly.

Pot traduir...? – Can you translate...?
Pot escriure...? – Can you write...?
Ho pot lletrejar? – Can you spell that?

Ho pot repitir, si us plau?
Can you please repeat that?

Què ha dit? – What did you say?

Com s'escriu això? – How do you write it?

Com es diu? – How do you say it?

Com es diu... en català?
How do you say....in Catalan?

Com es diu...en anglès?
How do you say...in English?

Com es diu...en castellà?
How do you say...in Spanish?

Com es pronuncia....?
How do you pronounce...?

La gent i les presentacions
(people and introductions)

dir-se – to be called/to be named

jo **em dic**… – my name is…

tu **et dius**… – your name is…(familiar)
vostè **es diu** – you namre is…(formal)

ell **es diu**… – his name is…
ella **es diu**… – her name is…

nosaltres **ens diem**… – our names are…

vosaltres **us dieu**… – your names are…(familiar)
vostès **es diuen** – your names are…(formal)

ells/elles **es diuen**… – their names are…

Com et dius? – What's your name? (familiar)
Com es diu (vostè)? – What's your name? (formal)
Em dic... – My name's...

Com es diu (ell)? – What's his name?
Com es diu (ella)? – What's her name?
Es diu... – His/Her name's...

ser – to be

jo **sóc** – I am

tu **ets** – you are (familiar)
vostè **és** – you are (formal)

ell **és** – he is
ella **és** – she is

nosaltres **som** – we are

vosaltres **sou** – you all are (familiar)
vostès **són** – you all are (formal)

ells **són** – they are (m.)*
elles **són** – they are (f.)*

Qui ets? – Who are you? (familiar)
Qui és vostè? – Who are you? (formal)

Qui és ell/ella? – Who is he/she?

Qui sou? – Who are you all? (familiar)
Qui són vostès? – Who are you all? (formal)

Qui són ells/elles?* – Who are they?

*In Catalan (the same as in Spanish), you can only use they feminine plural pronoun *elles* (or corresponding adjective form) when referring to more than one person or a group of people who are **all females** (also nouns that are feminine like *cases*). When referring to a mixed group of people (male and female) or objects of both genders, you must use the masculine plural pronoun *ells* or its corresponding adjective form.

Sóc (el) Francesc. – I'm Francis.
Sóc (en) Carles. – I'm Charles.
Sóc (l') Enric. – I'm Henry.
Sóc (la) Carme. – I'm Carmen.
Sóc (l') Anna. – I'm Anna.

Note: In many parts of Catalonia (but apparently **not** in Valencia) the definite articles *el*, *la* and *l'* are used before a person's first name (*en* is also sometimes used in front of a masculine first name). Likewise *el* and *la* are often used in front of *senyor* (Mr.) and *senyora* (Mrs.) followed by a surname. This does **not** occur when speaking directly to the person or in the **Em dic...** (My name is...) construction. For example:

Ets el Rafel? –Are you Ralph?
No, sóc l'Enric. - No, I'm Henry.
Ella és la Montse. – She's Montse.

however,

Em dic Vicent. – My name's Vincent. (*el*, *en*, *la* and *l'* not used with this construction)

Vicent, vine aquí! – Vincent, come here! (speaking directly to him)

Els possessius
(possessives)

el meu/la meva - my (singular)
els meus/les meves - my (plural)

el teu/la teva - your (singular)
els teus/les teves - your (plural)

el seu/la seva - his/her/its/their (singular)
els seus/les seves - his/her/its/their (plural)

el nostre/la nostra – our (singular)
els nostres/les nostres – our (plural)

el vostre/la vostra – your
(singular – when referring to more than one person)

els vostres/les vostres – your
(plural – when referring to more than one person)

Et (Li)* presento el meu pare.
I'd like you to meet my father.
Et (Li) presento la meva mare.
Let me introduce you to my mother.
Et (Li) presento els meus germans.
I'd like you to meet my brothers/siblings.
Et (Li) presento les meves germanes.
Let me introduce you to my sisters.

Us (Els)* presento el meu amic, (l')Eduard.
I'd like you all to meet my friend, Edward.

Us (Els) presento la meva amiga, (la) Laura.
I'd like you all to meet my friend, Laura.

Us (Els) presento els meus veïns...
I'd like you all to meet my neighbors (m. or m./f.)

Us (Els) presento les meves veïnes...
I'd like you all to meet my neighbors (all females).

Molt de gust. – Nice to meet you.

Encantat. (male speaker) - Delighted.

Encantada.(female speaker) - Delighted.

Igualment. – Likewise./Same here.

*Use *Li* and *Els* when introducing people to a person or persons with whom you would prefer to use the formal rather than the familiar.

La família

bebé/criatura – baby/infant
nen(a)/infant/criatura – infant

nen – child (m.)
nena – child (f.)

noi/xicot/mosso – boy
noia/xicota/mossa – girl

xicot – boyfriend
xicota – girlfriend

home – man
dona – woman

espòs/marit – spouse (m.)/husband
esposa/dona – spouse (f.)/wife

avi – grandfather/grandpa
àvia – grandmother/grandma

besavi – great grandfather
besàvia – great grandmother

rebesavi/tresavi – great great grandfather
rebesàvia/tresàvia – great great grandmother

nèt - grandson
nèta – granddaughter

pare – father
padrì/compare – godfather
padrastre – stepfather
sogre – father-in-law

mare – mother
padrina/comare – godmother
madrastra - stepmother
sogra – mother-in-law

fill – son
fillastre – stepson
fillol – godson

filla – daughter
fillastra – stepdaughter
fillola – goddaughter

gendre – son-in-law
nora – daughter-in-law

germà - brother
germanastre – stepbrother

germana – sister
germanastra – stepsister

cunyat – brother-in-law
cunyada – sister-in-law

oncle – uncle
tia – aunt

cosí – cousin (m.)
cosina – cousin (f.)

nebot – nephew
neboda – niece

Les professions

Què fa vostè?
Què treball té vostè?
Què fa vostè de treball?
Quin és el treball de vostè?
A què es dedica vostè?
What do you do for a living? (formal)

Què (treball*) fas?
Qué treball* tens?
Què feina* tens?
What do you do? (informal)
What's your job?

Sóc advocat. – I'm a lawyer.

Jo treballo en una oficina/un despatx.
I work in an office.

Jo treballo en una fàbrica.
I work in a factory.

*The word *el treball* is the normal word referring to work or a job. The informal equivalent is *la feina*.

Sóc... – I'm a(n)...

actor/actriu - actor/actress
advocat/advocada - lawyer
agricultor - farmer
alcalde – mayor
arquitecte - architect
atleta - athlete

banquer/banquera - banker
bomber – fireman

caixer/caixera - cashier
cambrer – waiter
cambrera – waitress, stewardess
cangur – babysitter (literally, *kangaroo*)
cantant - singer
cap - boss
capatàs/capatassa - foreman
carnisser/carnissera - butcher
carter/cartera – mail man/mail woman
científic/científica - scientist
comptable - accountant
cuiner/cuinera – cook

dependent/dependenta – shop assistant, sales clerk
dentista - dentist

enginyer - engineer
escriptor(a) – writer

forner/fornera - baker
fotògraf/fotògrafa - photographer
fuster – carpenter, joiner
futbolista – soccer player/footballer

gerent - manager

infermer/infermera - nurse

jugador(a) - player
jutge – judge

lampista/fontaner – plumber

mariner - sailor
mecànic/mecànica - mechanic
mestressa de casa – housewife/homemaker
metge/metgessa – doctor/physician
militar – soldier, serviceman
miner - miner
model - model
músic/música - musician

notari/notària - notary

obrer – worker, factory worker

pallasso/pallassa – clown
peó – unskilled worker
periodista – journalist
perruquer/perruquera – hairdresser, stylist
pilot - pilot

pintor(a) - painter
policia – police officer*
polític/política - politician

sacerdot - priest
secretari/secretària - secretary

soldat - soldier

xofer – chauffeur, driver

*Police officers are sometimes referred to *els mossos d'esquadra* in parts of Catalonia.

Lloc d' origen i residència
(place of origin and residence)

D'on ets? – Where are you from? (familiar)
D'on és vostè? – Where are you from? (formal)
Sóc de... – I'm from...

D'on sou? – Where are you all from? (familiar)
D'on són vostès? – Where are you all from? (formal)
Som de... – We're from...

D'on és ell? – Where is he from?
D'on és ella? – Where is she from?
És de... – He/She is from...

D'on són ells/elles? – Where are they from?
Són de... – They're from...

Les regions d' Espanya:
(the regions of Spain)

Andalusia - Andalusia
Aragó - Aragon
Astùries - Asturias
Cantàbria - Cantabria
Castella i Lleó - Castille and Leon
Catalunya – Catalonia
Comunitat de Madrid – The Community of Madrid
Extremadura – Extremadura
Galícia - Galicia

(les) Illes Balears – the Balearic Islands
(les) Illes Canàries – the Canary Islands
La Rioja - La Rioja
Mùrcia - Murcia
Navarra - Navarre
País Basc – The Basque Country
València - Valencia

Els països del món
(the countries of the world)

Àfrica
Algèria
Egipte
Líbia
Morroc
Tunísia

Europa
Alemanya (Germany)
Anglaterra
França
Itàlia
Rússia

Amèrica del Nord (North America)
Canadà
(els) Estats Units (the U.S.)
Mèxic

Amèrica del Sud (South America)
Bolívia
Colòmbia
Equador
Uruguai
Veneçuela
Xile

Àsia
Filipines
Japó
Xina

Oceania
Austràlia
Nova Zelanda

Els idiomes
(languages)

Parles...? – Do you speak...? (familiar)
Parla vostè...? - Do you speak…? (formal)

Parlo... - I speak...
No parlo...sinó... – I don't speak...but rather...

Parla ell...? – Does he speak...?
Parla ella...? – Does she speak...?
Parlen ells/elles...? – Do they speak...?

Parleu...? – Do you all speak...? (familiar)
Parlen (vostès)...? – Do you all speak...? (formal)

Parlem... – We speak...
Parlem..., però parlem també...
We speak..., but we also speak...

Parleu català?
Do you all speak Catalan? (familiar)

Vostès parlen català?
Do you all speak Catalan? (formal)

Sí, el parlem./Sí ho parlem.
Yes, we speak it.

No, no el parlem./No, no ho parlem.
No, we don't speak it.

No, nosaltres parlem anglès.
No, we speak English..

No parlem català, però parlem castellà.
We don't speak Catalan, but we speak Spanish.

Els idiomes del món/Les llengües del món
(the languages of the world)

alemany - German
anglès - English
castellà/espanyol - Spanish
català - Catalan
francès - French
grec - Greek
italià - Italian
japonès - Japanese
neerlandès - Dutch
noruec - Norwegian
polonès - Polish
portuguès - Portuguese
rus - Russian
turc - Turkish
suec - Swedish
txec - Czech
xinès - Chinese

The Verb *viure* and Cities

viure – to live

jo **visc** – I live

tu **vius** – you live
vostè viu – you live (formal9

ell/ella **viu** – he/she lives

nosaltres **vivim** – we live

vosaltres **viviu** – you all live
vostès viuen – you all live (formal)

ells/elles **viuen** – they live

On vius? – Where do you live? (familiar)
On viu vostè? – Where do you live? (formal)
Visc a... – I live in...

On viviu? – Where do you all live? (familiar)
On viuen (vostès)? – Where do you all live? (formal)
Vivim a... – We live in ...

On viu ell/ella? – Where does he/she live?
Viu a... – He/She lives in...

Les ciutats del món
(the cities of the world)

On viuen ells/elles? – Where do they live?
Viuen a... – They live in...

Alacant – Alicante
Atenes – Athens
Barcelona – Barcelona
Berlín – Berlin
Bons Aires – Buenos Aires
Brussel·les - Brussels
Ciutat de Mèxic – Mexico City
Dublín – Dublin
El Caire – Cairo
Estocolm – Stockholm
Florència – Florence
Ginebra – Geneva
Lisboa – Lisbon
Londres - London
Moscou – Moscow
Munic – Munich
Nàpols - Naples
Nova York – New York
París – Paris
Pequín – Bejing
Roma – Rome
Sant Petersburg – St. Petersburg
Singapur – Singapour
Seül – Seoul

Tòquio – Tokyo
Torì – Turin
València – Valencia
Varsòvia – Warsaw
Venècia – Venice
Viena – Vienna
Zuric – Zurich

El cos, la roba i les descripcions
(the body, clothes and descriptions)

The Verb *portar* and Clothing

jo **porto** – I wear, I'm wearing

tu **portes** – you wear, you're wearing (familiar)
vostè **porta** – you wear, are wearing (formal)

ell **porta** – he wears, he's wearing
ella **porta** – she wears, she's wearing

nosaltres **portem** – we wear, we're wearing

vosaltres **porteu** – you all wear/are wearing
vostès porten – you all wear, are wearing (formal)

ells/elles **porten** – they wear/are wearing

La roba (clothes)
l'**abric** – coat
el **barret** – hat
el **cinturó** – belt
el **guant** – glove
el **jersei/suèter** – sweater, pullover
el **vestit** – dress, suit
el **xandall** – tracksuit, sweatsuit

els **mitjons** – socks
els **pantalons** – pants/trousers
els **(pantalons) texans** – jeans

la **brusa** – blouse
la **bufanda** – scarf, muffler
la **camisa** – shirt
la **corbata** – tie
la **fadilla** – skirt
la **jaqueta** – jacket
la **llenceria** – lingerie
la **roba interior** – underwear
la **samarreta** – T-shirt

les **mitjanes** – pantyhose, tights
les **sabates** – shoes
les **sabatilles** – sneakers, trainers, house slippers
les **sandàlies** – sandals
les **ulleres** – glasses

Els adjectius per a descriure la roba
(adjectives used for describing clothing)

gran – big, large
petit, menut – little, small

llarg – long
curt – short

ample – wide, loose
estret – narrow, tight

net – clean
brut – dirty

mullat – wet
sec – dry

Example Sentences

El vestit és gran.
The dress is big.

El vestit és massa gran.
The dress is too big.

Aquest vestit és més gran que aquell vestit.
This dress is bigger than that dress.

Aquesta jaqueta és petita.
This jacket is small.

Aquesta jaqueta és massa petita.
This jacket is too small.

La meva jaqueta és més petita que la teva jaqueta.
My jacket is smaller than your jacket.

La meva és més petita que la teva.
Mine is smaller than yours.

Els colors
(colors)

blanc(a) – white
blau/blava – blue
castany – brown (hair)
gris(a) – gray/grey
groc/groga – yellow
marró – brown
negre/negra – black
roig(roja)/vermell(a) – red
rosa – pink
taronja – orange
verd(a) – green
violeta/lila – violet, purple

clar – light
fosc – dark

El gos és blanc. – The dog is white.
Els gossos són blancs. – The dogs are white.

L'ovella és blanca. – The sheep is white.
Les ovelles són blanques. – The sheep are white.

L'arbre és verd. – The tree is green.
Els arbres són verds. – The trees are green.

La fulla és verda. – The leaf is green.
Les fulles són verdes. – The leaves are green.

El cos humà
(the human body)

el **braç** – arm
el **cap** – head
el **coll** – neck
el **colze** – elbow
el **cor** – heart
el **dit** – finger
l'**estòmac** – stomach
el **fetge** – liver
el **front** – forehead
el **genoll** – knee
el **nas** – nose
el **pèl/cabell** – hair
el **peu** – foot
el **pit** – chest, breast
l'**ull** – eye
els **braços** – arms
els **canells** – wrists
els **dits** – fingers
els **pulmons** – lungs
els **ronyons** - kidneys
els **llavis** – lips
els **ulls** – eyes
la **boca** – mouth
la **cama** – leg
la **cara** – face
l'**esquena** – back
la **mà** – hand

l'**oïda** – inner ear
l'**orella** – outer ear
la **pell** – skin
la **sang** – blood
les **cames** – legs
les **dents** – teeth
les **espatlles** – shoulders
les **galtes** – cheeks
les **mans** – hands
les **oïdes** – inner ears
les **orelles** – outer ears

Ell/Ella *té*... – He/She has...

el **cabell llis/pèl llis*** – straight hair
el **cabell arrissat/pèl arrissat** – curly hair
el **cabell llarg/pèl llarg** – long hair
el **cabell curt/pèl curt** – short hair
el **pèl negre** – black hair
el **pèl castany** – brown hair
el **pèl ros** – blond hair
el **pèl roig** – red hair

*Notice that in Catalan, the adjective (*llis* in this case) usually goes after the noun. Adjectives occasionally go before the noun as in English, but much less frequently. Also: an alternative to the word *pèl* (hair) is *cabells* which requires the plural form of the adjective (e.g. *els cabells llisos*)

els **ulls marrons** – brown eyes
els **ulls verds** – green eyes
els **ulls blaus** – blue eyes

Example Sentences

Ell té un cap gran.
He has a big head.

El seu cap és gran.
His head is big.

Ella té una boca petita.
She has a small mouth.

La seva boca és petita.
Her mouth is small.

Ella té les cames llargues.
She has long legs.

Les seves cames són llargues.
Her legs are long.

Els dies, els mesos i les estacions
(days, months and seasons)

els dies de la setmana
(the days of the week)

dilluns – Monday
dimarts – Tuesday
dimecres – Wednesday
dijous – Thursday
divendres – Friday
dissabte – Saturday
diumenge – Sunday

Avui és dilluns.
Today is Monday.

Ahir va ser diumenge.
Yesterday was Sunday.

Demà és dimarts.
Tomorrow is Tuesday.

Els mesos de l'any
(the months of the year)

gener - January
febrer - February
març - March
abril - April
maig - May
juny - June
juliol - July
agost - August
septembre – September
octubre - October
novembre - November
desembre – December

L'escola comença al setembre.
School starts in September.

El Nadal és al desembre.
Christmas is in December.

Fa vent al març.
It's windy in March.

Plou molt a l'abril.
It rains a lot in April.

Les estacions de l'any
(the seasons of the year)

l'**hivern** – winter
la **primavera** – spring
l'**estiu** – summer
la **tardor** – autumn/fall

La tardor és la meva estació preferida.
The autumn is my favorite season.

Fa molt de fred a l'hivern.
It's really cold in the winter.

Hi ha moltes flors acolorides a la primavera.
There are lots of colorful flowers in the spring.

Fa molta calor a l'estiu.
It's really hot in the summer.

Els nombres
(numbers)

0 - zero
1 - u*
2 - dos/dues**
3 - tres
4 - quatre
5 - cinc
6 - sis
7 - set
8 - vuit
9 - nou
10 - deu
11 – onze
12 - dotze
13 - tretze
14 - catorze
15 - quinze
16 - setze
17 - disset
18 – divuit
19 - dinou
20 - vint
21 - vint-i-u
22 - vint-i-dos
23 - vint-i-tres

un and *una* before m. and f. nouns
**dues* before a feminine noun

24 – vint-i-quatre
25 – vint-i-cinc
26 – vint-i-sis
27 – vint-i-set
28 – vint-i-vuit
29 – vint-i-nou
30 – trenta
31 – trenta-u
40 – quaranta
50 – cinquanta
60 – seixanta
70 – setanta
80 – vuitanta
90 – noranta

100 – cent
101 – cent u*
102 – cent dos**

110 – cent deu
120 – cent vint

200 – dos-cents**
300 – tres-cents

un and *una* before m. and f. nouns
**dues* before a feminine noun

400 – quatre-cents
500 - cinc-cents
600 - sis-cents
700 - set-cents
800 – vuit-cents
900 - nou-cents

1,000 – mil
1,001 - mil u*
1,002 - mil dos**

2,000 - dos mil**

100,000 - cent mil

1,000,000 - un milió
2,000,000 - dos* milions

*un and una before m. and f. nouns
**dues before a feminine noun

Ordinal Numbers

<u>Els nombres ordinals</u>
1r/1ª - primer/primera (first)
2n/2ª - segon/segona (second)
3r/3ª - tercer/tercera (third)
4t/4ª - quart/quarta (fourth)
5é/5ª - cinqué/cinquena (fifth)
6é/6ª - sisé/sisena (sixth)
7é/7ª - seté/setena (seventh)
8é/8ª - vuité/vuitena (eighth)
9é/9ª - nové/novena (ninth)
10é/10a - desé/desena (tenth)

La data i altres paraules
(the date and other words)

Quina és la data d'avui?
What's the date today?
Avui es el 5(cinc) de març.
Today's March 5.*

ahir - yesterday
abans d'ahir – the day before yesterday
demà - tomorrow
demà passat – the day after tomorrow

aquesta setmana – this week
la setmana passada – last week
la pròxima setmana/la setmana que ve – next week

aquest mes – this month
el mes passat – last month
el pròxim mes/el mes que ve – next month

aquest any – this year
l'any passat – last year
el pròxim any/l'any que ve – next year

*Please note that in Catalan, normal numbers (cardinal numbers) are used to talk about the date rather than ordinal number (as in English). The only exception to this might be *el primer* (the first) to talk about the first day of the month.

Parlar de l'hora
(telling time)

Quina hora és? – What time is it?
Quina hora és, ara? – What time is it now?

(Que) tens hora?
Can you tell me the time? (familiar)

(Que) té hora?
Can you tell me the time? (formal)

És l'una. – It's 1:00.
És l'una i quart. – It's 1:15.
És l'una i mitja. – It's 1:30.

Són les dues. – It's 2:00.
Són les dues (i) cinc (minuts). – It's 2:05.
Són les tres (i) vint (minuts). – It's 3:20.
Són les quatre i mitja. – It's 4:30.
Són les sis menys quart. – It's quarter to six (5:45).

In the Past:

Era l'una. – It was one o'clock.
Eren les dues. – It was three o'clock.

A quina hora...? – At what time...?

A quina hora arriba el tren?
At what time does the train arrive?

A quina hora surt el vol?
At what time does the flight leave?

a l'una – at 1:00
a les dues – at 2:00
a les tres – at 3:00

del matí – in the morning
de la tarda – in the afternoon
de la nit/del vespre – in the evening

al migdia – at noon/at midday
a la mitjanit – at midnight

Quant dura...? – How long does...last?

una hora – an hour
dues hores – two hours

Telling Time the Catalan Way

Here's another way of telling time often used in Catalonia. This way is perhaps more complicated than the way I have shown in the previous page, which is more similar to the way of telling time in Spanish. If you use the simpler way, you will certainly be understood, even if Catalans prefer the other (and in my opinion, more complicated) method below. This method refers to quarter hours before the next hour. Therefore, *És un quart de sis* (literally *It's a quarter of six*) means that it's 5:15 (not 5:45!)

És un quart de sis. – It's 5:15.

Són dos quarts de sis. – It's 5:30.

Son tres quarts de sis. – It's 5:45.

És un quart i deu (minuts) de vuit. – It's 7:25.

Són dos quarts i cinc (minuts) de vuit. – It's 7:35.

Les activitats i els llocs
(activities and places)

(a mi) **m'agrada** – I like

(a tu) **t'agrada** – you like (familiar)
(a vostè) li agrada – you like (formal)

(a ell) **li agrada** – he likes
(a ella) **li agrada** – she likes

(a nosaltres) **ens agrada** – we like

(a vosaltres) **us agrada** – you all like (familiar)
(a vostès) els agrada – you all like (formal)

(a ells) **els agrada** – they like (m.)
(a elles) **els agrada** – they like (f.)

M'**agrada** aquest vi. – I like this wine.
M'**agraden** aquests vins. – I like these wines.

acampar/anar a càmping – to camp, go camping
ajudar – to help
anar a comprar – to go shopping
aprendre – to learn
ballar – to dance
berenar – to have an afternoon snack
beure – to drink
cavalcar – to ride a horse

caminar – to walk
caminar amb el gos – to walk the dog
cantar – to sing
compartir – to share
córrer – to run
dibuixar – to draw
dinar –to eat, have lunch
ensenyar – to teach
esmorzar – to have breakfast
escoltar música – to listen to music
escriure els emails als meus amics – to write e-mails to my friends
esquiar – to ski
estudiar – to study
experimentar – to experience/experiment
explorar – to explore
fer el muntanyisme – to go mountain-climbing
fer la gimnàstica – to exercise/work out
jugar – to play (sports or games)
llegir els llibres – to read books
llegir les novel·les – to read novels
llegir el periòdic – to read the newspaper
llegir les revistes – to read magazines
menjar – to eat
muntar a cavall – to ride horses
muntar a bicicleta – to cycle, ride bikes

nedar – to swim
parlar amb els amics
to talk with my friends (m.)
parlar amb les amigues
to talk with my friends (f.)
passar el temps amb…
to spend time with…
passejar – to go for a walk/stroll
patinar – to skate
pintar – to paint
practicar els esports – to practice sport(s)
preparar – to prepare
rebre regals – to receive gifts
sopar – to have supper
tocar – to play music
treballar – to work
veure la televisió – to watch tv

veure els programes de cuinar
to watch cooking programs

veure els programes de noticies
to watch news programs

veure els programes de la història
to watch history programs

veure els programes culturals
to watch cultural programs

veure les sèries – to watch tv series

veure les sèries gracioses/còmiques
to watch comedy series/sit-coms

viatjar – to travel
viure – to live

The Verb *anar* (to go) and *els llocs* (places)

anar (to go)

jo **vaig** – I go, I'm going

tu **vas** – you go, you're going (familiar)
vostè **va** – you go, you're going (formal)

ell **va** – he goes, he's going
ella **va** – she goes, she's going

nosaltres **anem** – we go, we're going

vosaltres **aneu** – you all go, are going (fam.)
vostès **van** – you all go, are going (formal)

ells **van** – they go, they're going (m.)
elles **van** – they go, they're going (f.)

Vaig* a dinar. – I'm going to have lunch.
Anem a veure la televisió. – We're going to watch tv.

*Remember that –ig (at the end of a word) is pronounced like *sh* or *ch* in the word *church*.

Anem... – We're going...
a l'ajuntament – to the town hall
al banc – to the bank
al bar – to the bar
al barri – to the neighborhood
al bosc – to the forest/woods
al bulevar – to the boulevard
al cafè – to the café
al camp – to the field/to the country
al carrer – to the street
al castell – to the castle
al centre – downtown, to the city center
al cinema – to the cinema, movies
al concert – to the concert
a correus – to the post office
al despatx – to the office
a l'estadi – to the stadium
al gimnàs – to the gym
a l'hospital – to the hospital
a l'hotel – to the hotel
al llac – to the lake
al mercat – to the market
al palau – to the palace
al parc – to the park
al restaurant – to the restaurant
al riu – to the river
al taller – to the workshop/repair shop

al teatre – to the theater
al treball – to work
a l'avinguda – to the avenue
a la botiga – to the store/shop
a la cafeteria – to the cafeteria
a la carnisseria – to the butcher's shop
a la catedral – to the cathedral
a la cita – to the appointment/date
a la ciutat – to the city/to town
a la discoteca – to the disco
a l'escola – to (the) school
a l'església – to the church
a l'estació – to the station
a la farmàcia – to the pharmacy, drugstore, chemist's
a la festa – to the party
a la fleca – to the bakery
a la fruiteria – to the fruit shop/greengrocer's
a la missa – to (the) mass
a l'oficina – to the office
a la desfilada – to the parade
a la pastisseria – to the pastry shop
a la peixateria – to the fish shop/fishmonger's
a la piscina – to the swimming pool
a la plaça – to the town square
a la platja – to the beach
a la reunió – to the meeting, get-together
a la universitat – to the university

Here is a way that sometimes people refer to someone's "place", perhaps similar to *chez* in French:

casa - house
ca – the house of/…'s place

cal – the house of (of man)
cal Josep – Joseph's house/place

cals – the house of (more than one person)
cals pares – my parents' house/place

can – the house of a man or woman...
can Lluís – Louis's house/place

ca l' – the house of a man or woman whose name begins with a vowel
ca l'Enric – Henry's house/place
ca l'Anna – Anna's house/place

ca la - the house of (a woman)
ca la Montse – Montse's house/place

ca les – the house of (more than one woman)
ca les cosines – my (female) cousins' house/place

Demanar les indicacions
(asking for directions)

Disculpi. – Excuse me. (formal)
Disculpa. – Excuse me. (informal)

On és...? – Where is...?
On són...?/ – Where are...?

Com es pot arrivar allà?
How can I get there?

Estic perdut. – I'm lost. (m.)
Estic perduda. – I'm lost. (f.)

Estem perduts. – We're lost.(m.,m/f)
Estem perdudes. – We're lost. (f.)

Seguiu.../Vagi... – Continue.../Go...
Giri... – Turn...

des (de)... – from...(lit. *since*)
fins (a)... – until.../to...
cap (a)... – towards...

endavant – ahead/straight on
dret/tot recte.... – straight (ahead)

Passi.../Vostè va a passar... – You'll pass...

la dreta – right
a la dreta/a mà dreta – on the right (hand side)

l'esquerra – left
a l'esquerra/a la mà esquerra – on the left

davant (de) – in front of
darrere (de) – behind
al costat (de) – beside, next to

a prop – near, close to
lluny – far (from)

És lluny. – It's far.
No és lluny. – It isn't far.

Vostè veurà... – You'll see...

l'**angle** – the angle, corner
el **camí** – the way, route, street
el **carrer** – the street, road
el **mapa** – the map
el **peatge** – the toll booth
el **semàfor** – the traffic light
el **senyal** – the sign, indication

l'**autopista** – the highway/motorway
l'**autovia** – the highway/motorway
l'**avinguda** – the avenue
la **cantonada** – the corner
l'**estació** – the station
la **placa de carrer** – the street sign
la **plaça** – the square, plaza
la **sortida** – the exit, way out

a la **cantonada** – to the (on the) corner

al **primer carrer** – to the (on the) first street
al **segon carrer** – to the second street
al **tercer carrer** – to the third street
al **quart carrer** – to the fourth street

Els mitjans de transport
(means of transport)

Cal agafar... – You must take...

l'**autobús**/el **bus** – bus
l'**avió** – plane
el **camió** – truck/lorry
el **cotxe** – car
el **metro** – subway/underground
el **taxi** – taxi
el **tramvia** – tram/trolley
el **tren** – train
el **vaixell**/la **nau** – ship

la **barca** – boat
la **bicicleta** – bike
la **moto** – motorbike

Vaig... – I go, I'm going...
Vinc... – I come, I'm coming...
Arribo... – I arrive, I'm arriving...
Viatjo... – I travel, I'm travelling...

amb cotxe – by car
amb taxi – by taxi
amb tren – by train

El pronòstic del temps
(talking about the weather)

fer – to do, make

jo **faig*** – I do, I make

tu **fas** – you do, you make
vostè fa – you do, you make

ell **fa** – he does, he makes
ella **fa** – she does, she makes

nosaltres **fem** – we do, we make

vosaltres **feu** – you all do, make (familiar)
vostès **fan** – you all do, make (formal)

ells **fan** – they do, they make (m.)
elles **fan** – they do, they make (f.)

Quin temps fa? – What's the weather like?

Fa bo./Fa bon temps. – It's nice weather.

Fa fred. – It's cold.
Fa calor. – It's hot.

*Remember that –ig (at the end of a word) is pronounced like *sh* or the *ch* of *church*.

Fa vent. – It's windy.
Fa sol. – It's sunny.

Hi ha boira. – It's foggy.
Hi ha tempesta. – It's stormy.

Hi ha núvols./Està núvol./Està cobert.
It's cloudy./It's overcast.

Hi ha humitat. – It's humid.

Plou. – It rains. (in general)
Està plovent. – It's raining. (at this moment)

Neva. – It snows. (in general)
Està nevant. – It's snowing. (at this moment)

House and Home

La casa (the house/home)
l'**armari** – closet (US)/wardrobe (UK)
el **bany** – bathroom
el **calaix** – drawer
el **clau** – nail
el **cristall** – glass
el **garatge** – garage
el **jardí** – garden
el **llit** – bed
el **llum** – light, lamp, light source
el **menjador** – dining room
el **maó** – brick
el **mirall** – mirror
el **moble** – piece of furniture
el **pal de fregar** – mop
el **passadís/corredor** – hall/corridor
el **pis** – apartment, flat, storey
el **quadre** – painting
el **racó** – corner
el **saló** – living room
el **sofà** – sofa/couch
el **sostre** – ceiling
el **televisor** – television set
el **terra** – floor
els **cristalls** – window panes
els **maons** – bricks
els **mobles** – furniture
els **quadres** – paintings

la **banyera** – bathtub
la **cadira** – chair
la **catifa** – rug
la **clau** – key
la **cortina** – curtain
la **cuina** – kitchen
la **cambra** – bedroom
l'**escombra** – broom
la **finestra** – window
la **flor** – flower
la **fusta** – wood
la **gespa** – lawn
la **habitació** – room
la **làmpada**/el **llum** – lamp
la **llum** – light (natural)
la **paret** – wall
la **planta** – plant
la **porta** – door
la **sala** – living room
la **taula** - table
les **cadires** – chairs
les **cortines** – curtains
les **claus** – keys
les **flors** – flowers
les **persianes** – blinds, metal window covers
les **plantes** – plants

escombrar – to sweep
l'escombra – the broom

fregar – to mop
el pal de fregar – the mop

rentar els plats – to wash the dishes

rentar la roba – to do the laundry/wash clothes
fer la bugada – to do laundry (informal9

netejar – to clean
ordenar – to straighten, tidy

passar l'aspiradora – to vacuum, to hoover
l'aspiradora – vacuum cleaner, hoover

planxar – to iron

treure les escombraries
to take out the trash/rubbish

treure la pols – to dust

Animals and Nature

Veig... – I see...
Puc veure... – I can see...

Veiem... – We see...
Podem veure... – We can see...

Allà hi ha... – There is/There I see...

els animals
l'**ànec** – duck
el **cavall** – horse
el **cocodril** – crocodile
el **conill** – rabbit
el **dofí** – dolphin
l'**elefant** – elephant
l'**estruç** – ostrich
el **gat** – cat
el **gall** – rooster/cockerel
el **gos** – dog
el **guineu** – fox
el **llop** – wolf
el **lleó** – lion
l'**ocell** – bird
l'**òs** – bear
el **peix** – fish
el **porc** – pig
el **tauró** – shark
el **tigre** – tiger

l'**abella** – bee
la **balena** – whale
la **cabra** – goat
la **gallina** – hen
la **granota** – frog
la **mosca** – fly
l'**oca** – goose
l'**ovella** – sheep
la **serp** – snake, serpent
la **tortuga** – turtle, tortoise
la **vaca** – cow

El gos és bonic.
The dog is cute.

El gosset és bonic.
The little dog is cute.

El gat és grotesc.
The cat is grotesque.

El lleó és valent.
The lion is brave.

El lleó no és covard.
The lion is not cowardly.
The lion is no coward.

La naturalesa
(nature)

Veig... – I see...
Puc veure... – I can see...

Veiem... – We see...
Podem veure... – We can see...

Allà hi ha... – There is/There I see...

l'**arbre** – tree
el **bosc** – forest/woods
el **camp** – field, country
el **desert** – desert
l'**estel** – star
el **gel** – ice
el **llac** – lake
el **mar** – sea (also *la mar*)
el **núvol** – cloud
l'**oceà** – ocean
el **parc** – park
el **riu** – river
el **sol** – sun
el **vent** – wind
els **estels** – stars
els **núvols** – clouds
l'**estrella** – star
la **flor** – flower
la **fulla** – leaf

l'**herba** – grass
la **lluna** – moon
la **muntanya** – mountain
la **neu** – snow
l'**onada** – wave
la **platja** – beach
la **pluja** – rain
la **selva** – jungle
la **sorra** – sand
les **estrelles** – stars
les **flors** – flowers
les **fulles** – leaves
les **muntanyes** – mountains
les **onades** – waves
les **plantes** – plants

Les flors floreixen a la primavera.
The flowers blossom in the spring.

Sempre vaig a les muntanyes a l'estiu.
I always go to the mountains in the summer.

L'arbre és gegantí.
The tree is gigantic.

El llac és enorme.
The lake is enormous.

Els aliments i les begudes
(food and drinks)

menjar (to eat)
jo *menjo* – I eat
tu *menges* – you eat
vostè *menja* – you eat (formal)
ell *menja* – he eats
ella *menja* – she eats
nosaltres *mengem* – we eat
vosaltres *mengeu* – you all eat
vostès *mengen* – you all eat (formal)
ells/elles *mengen* – they eat

prendre (to take, eat or drink)
jo *prenc* – I take
tu *prens* – you take
vostè *pren* – you take (formal)
ell *pren* – he takes
ella *pren* – she takes
nosotros *prenem* – we take
vosaltres *preneu* – you all take
vostès *prenen* – you all take (formal)
ells/elles *prenen* – they take

servir (to serve)
jo *serveixo* – I serve
tu *serveixes* – you serve
vostè *serveix* – you serve (formal)
ell *serveix* – he serves

ella *serveix* – she serves
nosaltres *servim* – we serve
vosaltres *serviu* – you all serve
vostès *serveixen* – you all serve (formal)
ells/elles *serveixen* – they serve

demanar (to ask, ask for, order)
jo *demano* – I order
tu *demanes* – you order
vostè *demana* – you order
ell *demana* – he orders
ella *demana* – she orders
nosaltres *demanem* – we order
vosaltres *demaneu* – you all order
vostès *demanen* – you all order (formal)
ells/elles *demanen* – they order

M'agradaria demanar, si us plau.
I'd like to order, please.

Ens agradaria demanar, si us plau.
We'd like to order, please.

Vol(s) prendre alguna cosa?
Would you like to eat or drink something?*

Què vol(s) beure?
What would you like to drink?*

Què vol(s) picar?
What would you like for starters?*

Vol(s) prendre alguna cosa?
Would you like to eat or drink something

Pot(s) cobrar?
May I pay? (lit. Can you charge me?)*

M'agradaria... – I'd like...
Ens agradaria... – We'd like...

Si us plau... – Please...

Em pot(s) portar...? – Can you bring me...?
Ens pot(s) portar...? – Can you bring us...?

El compte, si us plau.
The check/bill, please.

---

*Remember that the only difference between the verb forms *vol/vols* and *pot/pots* is that the form that ends with the *s* is the familiar form and the form without the *s* is the formal form. Therefore, you would use *vols* and *pots* with friends, people younger than you or people you know well and *vol* and *pot* with others. Waiters and waitresses may address you either way depending on your age or if they know you or not.

l'**all** – garlic
l'**allioli** – garlic and olive oil mayonnaise
l'**ànec** – duck
l'**arròs** – rice
el **bacallà** – cod
el **berenar** – afternoon snack
el **cafè** – coffee
el **cafè amb llet** – coffee made with warm milk
el **carajillo/cigaló** – coffee with liquor
el **compte** – the bill/check (at a restaurant)
el **conill** – rabbit
el **croissant** – croissant
el **dinar** – lunch, main afternoon meal
l'**entrepà** – sandwich, snack
el **ganivet** – knife
l'**enciam** – lettuce
l'**esmorzar** – breakfast
el **flam** – flan, a caramel custard dessert
el **formatge** – cheese
el **gelat** – ice cream
el **got** – glass
el **llenguado** – sole/flounder
el **lluç** – hake (a white fish)
el **menjar** – food, meal
el **nap** – turnip
l'**oli d'oliva** – olive oil
el **pa** – bread

el **pa tomàquet** – bread rubbed with fresh tomato and seasoned with olive oil and salt; sometimes eaten as is or used for making sandwiches
el **pastís** – pie, cake, pastry
el **pebre** – black table pepper
el **peix** – fish
el **pernil** – ham
el **plat** – plate
el **plàtan** – banana
el **pollastre** – chicken
el **porc** – pork
el **pot** – jar
el **préssec** – peach
el **sandvitx** – sandwich
el **refresc** – soft drink
el **sopar** – supper, evening dinner
el **suc** – juice
el **sucre** – sugar
el **tall de...** – the slice of...
el **tallat** – café espresso with a bit of milk
el **te** – tea
el **te amb llimona** – tea with lemon
el **tomàquet** – tomato
el **tovalló** – napkin, serviette
el **vi blanc** – white wine
el **vi negre** – red wine (lit. *black wine*)

el **vinagre** – vinegar
el **xai** – lamb
els **bolets/xampinyons** – mushrooms
els **calamars** – squid
els **espàrrecs** – asparagus
els **embotits** – sausages used for sandwich meat
els **macarrons** – macaroni
els **ous** – eggs
els **pésols** – peas
els **raïms** – grapes

l'**aigua** – water
l'**amanida** – salad
l'**ampolla** – bottle
la **botifarra** – traditional Catalonian link sausage
la **carn** – meat
la **ceba** – onion
la **cervesa** – beer
la **cullera** – spoon
l'**emsaïmada** – sweet bun
la **farina** – flour
la **figa** – fig
la **forquilla** – fork
la **infusió** – herbal tea
la **llauna** – can/tin
la **llet** – milk

la **llimona** – lemon
la **maduixa** – strawberry
la **mel** – honey
la **melmelada** – jam
la **mahonesa** – mayonnaise
la **mostassa** – mustard
l'**oliva** – olive
la **pera** – pear
la **pasta** – pasta or breakfast pastry
la **pastanaga** – carrot
la **pinya** - pineapple
la **poma** - apple
la **sal** - salt
la **sopa** - soup
la **tapa** – hors d'œuvre, bar snack
la **taronja** – orange
la **tassa** – cup
la **tomata** – tomato
la **tonyina** – tuna
la **truita** – trout
la **truita d'ou** – omelette
la **vedella** - veal
la **xocolata** – chocolate

les **anxoves** - anchovies
les **cireres** - cherries
les **fruites** – fruit(s)
les **gambes** – shrimp (US)/prawns (UK)
les **patates** – potatoes
les **postres** – dessert(s)
les **verdures** – vegetables

Basic Grammar

The six verb forms in Catalan correspond to the following pronouns:

1. **jo** (I)
2. **tu** (you – familiar)
3. **ell** (he), **ella** (she), **vostè** (you-formal)
4. **nosaltres** (we)
5. **vosaltres** (you all – familiar)
6. **ells** (they-m.), **elles** (they-f.), **vostès** (you all – formal)

Regular Verbs in the Present Tense
(I speak, I'm speaking, I do speak)

Regular AR Verbs are regular verbs whose infinitive form ends with –ar. You must remove the –ar ending before adding the following verb form endings (you will do the same with ER/RE and IR verbs):

parlar (to speak)
jo parl**o**
tu parl**es**
ell/ella parl**a**

nosaltres parl**em**
vosaltres parl**eu**
ells/elles parl**en**

Other important AR verbs:

agafar – to catch, take (e.g. a train), grasp, hold
buscar – to look for
caminar – to walk
canviar – to change, exchange
comprar – to buy
comptar – to count, tell, recount
cridar – to scream, shout
cuinar – to cook
dibuixar – to draw
donar – to give
escoltar – to hear, listen (to)
estimar – to love
enviar – to send
gastar (diners) – to spend (money)
ficar – to put, to put in(side)
menjar – to eat, have a meal**
mirar – to watch, look at
netejar – to clean**
passar – to pass
passar el temps – to spend time
perdonar – to forgive
pintar – to paint
plorar – to cry, weep
portar – to bring, carry, wear
posar – to put

pujar – to go up, get on (e.g. a bike, train)**
rentar – to wash
tornar – to return
treballar – to work
trencar – to break*
triar – to choose, elect
trobar – to find
trucar – to call, phone (CA)
viatjar – to travel**

*c→qu before e, e.g. busques, busquem)
**j→g before e, e.g. puges, pugem

Regular ER/RE Verbs
perdre (to lose)
jo perd**o**
tu perd**s**
ell/ella *perd*

nosaltres perd**em**
vosaltres perd**eu**
ells/elles perd**en**

Other regular ER/RE verbs:

batre – to beat, hit, strike
témer – to fear

Regular IR Verbs
dormir (to sleep)
jo dorm**o**
tu dorm**s**
ell/ella *dorm*

nosaltres dorm**im**
vosaltres dorm**iu**
ells/elles dorm**en**

Here are some other regular IR verbs:

morir – to die
obrir – to open
sentir – to feel, regret
sortir – to leave, go out

There is a second category of IR verbs which follow the pattern of the verb *preferir:*

preferir (to prefer)
jo prefer**eixo**
tu prefer**eixes**
ell/ella prefer**eix**
nosaltres prefer**im**
vosaltres prefer**iu**
ells/elles prefer**eixen**

Other verbs in this category:

decidir – to decide
llegir – to read
oferir – to offer
patir – to suffer
servir – to serve

The Simple Past

The Simplest Simple Past Tense – There *is* a more complicated past tense. However, I will teach you the simplest one which is simply to use the helping verb *anar* (to go) with the infinitve form of the verb. The verb forms of the helping verb *anar* only differ from the normal verb *anar* on forms 4 and 5 which are *vam* and *vau* respectively. For example:

jo *vaig* parlar – I spoke
tu *vas* parlar – you spoke
el/ella *va* parlar – he/she spoke
nosaltres *vam* parlar – we spoke
vosaltres *vau* parlar – you all spoke
ells/elles *van* parlar – they spoke

Please don't confuse this past tense construction with the **going to + infinitive** construction which always uses the preposition *a* and the regular 4 and 5 forms *anem* and *aneu* respectively. For example:

jo *vaig a* parlar – I'm going to speak
tu *vas a* parlar – you're going to speak
ell/ella *va a* parlar – he/she is going to speak
nosaltres *anem a* parlar – we're going to speak
vosaltres *aneu a* parlar – you all are going to speak
ells/elles *van a* parlar – they're going to speak

The Imperfect Tense
(I spoke, I was speaking, I used to speak)

Regular AR Verbs

parlar

jo parl**ava**
tu parl**aves**
ell/ella parl**ava**

nosaltres parl**àvem**
vosaltres parl**àveu**
ells/elles parl**aven**

Regular ER/RE/IR Verbs (they all have the same endings)

perdre

jo perd**ia**
tu perd**ies**
ell/ella perd**ia**

nosaltres perd**íem**
vosaltres perd**íeu**
ells/elles perd**ien**

The Present Perfect
(I have spoken)

This tense is formed using the helping verb **haver** and the past participle.

parlar→*parlat*
perdre→*perdut*
dormir→*dormit*

jo **he** parlat – I have spoken
tu **has** parlat – you have spoken
ell/ella **ha** parlat – he/she has spoken

nosaltres **hem** parlat – we have spoken
vosaltres **heu** parlat – you all have spoken
ells/elles **han** parlat – they have spoken

The past perfect is formed the same way, but using the past forms of haver (*havia, havies, havia, havíem, havíeu, havien*). The following verbs have irregular past participles:

aprendre (to learn): *après*
beure (to drink): *begut*
caure (to fall): *caigut*
córrer (to run): *corregut*
creure (to believe): *cregut*
escriure (to write): *escrit*
fer (to do, make): *fet*

obrir (to open): *obert*
ploure (to rain): *plogut*
poder (to be able, can): *pogut*
prendre (to take): *pres*
riure (to laugh): *rigut*
tenir/tindre (to have): *tingut*
valer (to be worth): *valgut*
vendre (to sell): *venut*
venir/vindre (to come): *vingut*
veure (to see): *vist*
viure (to live): *viscut*
voler (to want): *volgut*

The Future Tense and Conditional Mood

The future tense (I will speak) and the conditional mood (I would speak) are formed by adding their respective verb form endings to the **infinitve form*** of the verb, and they will use the same ending for all verbs. Please note that the conditional endings are the same as the imperfect endings for ER/RE/IR verbs.

jo parlar**é** – I will speak
tu parlar**às** - you will speak
ell/ella parlar**à** – he/she will speak
nosaltres parlar**em** – we will speak
vosaltres parlar**eu** – you all will speak
ells/elles parlar**an** – they will speak

jo parlar**ia** – I would speak
tu parlar**ies** - you would speak
ell/ella parlar**ia** – he/she would speak
nosaltres parlar**íem** – we would speak
vosaltres parlar**íeu** – you all would speak
ells/elles parlar**ien** – they would speak

*with the exception of some verbs which use an irregular stem in lieu of the infinitive, for example:

anar (to go) →*anir-*
fer (to do, make) →*far-*
poder (to be able) →*podr-*
saber (to know) →*sabr-*
tenir (to have) →*tindr-*
venir (to come) →*vindr-*
voler (to want) →*voldr-*

Irregular Verbs in the Present Tense

Irregular Verbs – Verbs that do not follow the regular patterns mentioned above are considered *irregular*. We have already seen the following irregular verbs:

anar – to go
fer – to do, make
ser/estar (to be)
tenir (to have)
viure (to live)

Here are some others which you will likely encounter:

aprendre (to learn)
jo *aprenc*
tu *aprens*
ell/ella *aprèn*
nosaltres *aprenem*
vosaltres *apreneu*
ells/elles *aprenen*

beure (to drink)
jo *bec*
tu *beus*
ell/ella *beu*
nosaltres *bevem*
vosaltres *beveu*
ell/elles *beuen*

caure (to fall)
jo *caic*
tu *caus*
ell/ella *cau*
nosaltres *caiem*
vosaltres *caieu*
ells/elles *cauen*

creure (to believe)
jo *crec*
tu *creus*
ell/ella *creus*
nosaltres *creiem*
vosaltres *creieu*
ells/elles *creuen*

deure (to owe, ought to, must)
jo *dec*
tu *deus*
ell/ella *deu*
nosaltres *devem*
vosaltres *deveu*
ell/elles *deuen*

dir (to say, tell)
jo *dic*
tu *dius*
ell/ella *diu*
nosaltres *diem*
vosaltres *dieu*
ells/elles *diuen*

dur (to carry, take, wear)
jo *duc*
tu *duus* (also *dus*)
ell/ella *duu* (also *du*)
nosaltres *duem*
vosaltres *dueu*
ells/elles *duen*

escriure (to write)
jo *escric*
tu *escrius*
ell/ella *escriu*
nosaltres *escrivim*
vosaltres *escriviu*
ells/elles *escriuen*

poder (to be able, can)
jo *puc*
tu *pots*
ell/ella *pot*
nosaltres *podem*
vosaltres *podeu*
ells/elles *poden*

prendre (to take)
jo *prenc*
tu *prens*
ell/ella *pren*
nosaltres *prenem*
vosaltres *preneu*
ells/elles *prenen*

saber (to know)
jo *sé*
tu *saps*
ell/ella *sap*
nosaltres *sabem*
vosaltres *sabeu*
ells/elles *saben*

venir (to come)
jo *vinc*
tu *véns*
ell/ella *ve*
nosaltres *venim*
vosaltres *veniu*
ells/elles *vénen*

veure (to see)
jo *veig*
tu *veus*
ell/ella *veu*
nosaltres *veiem*
vosaltres *veieu*
ells/elles *veuen*

voler (to want, wish)
jo *vull*
tu *vols*
ell/ella *vol*
nosaltres *volem*
vosaltres *voleu*
ells/elles *volen*

Els adjectius
(adjectives)

Here I will list the four forms of the following adjectives which correspond to:
m. singular, f. singular, m. plural, f. plural.

Regular Adjectives:
verd, verda, verds, verdes (green)
net, neta, nets, netes (clean)
brut, bruta, bruts, brutes (dirty, ugly)
savi, sàvia, savis, sàvies (wise)

Adjectives ending in –s, -ç, -x, -ix, –tx:
gris, grisa, grisos, grises (gray/grey)
dolç, dolça, dolços, dolces (sweet)
fix, fixa, fixos, fixes (fixed, definite)
baix, baixa, baixos, baixes (short, low)

Some adjectives ending with s double the s:
gros, grossa, grossos, grosses (fat, thick, large)

Adjectives ending –sc, -st, -xt, -ig have two possible m. plural forms:

fresc, fresca, frescs/frescos, fresques (cool, fresh)
trist, trista, trists/tristos, tristes (sad)
mixt, mixta, mixts/mixtos, mixtes (mixed)
lleig, lletja, lleigs/lletjos, lletges (ugly)

c → g/gu:
groc, groga, grocs, grogues (yellow)
c → qu/qü:
oblic, obliqua, oblics, obliqües (oblique)
ç → c:
audaç, audaç, audaços, audaces (audacious)

t → d:
menut, menuda, menuts, menudes (small)
ig → j/g:
roig, roja, rojos/roigs, roges (red)
ig → tj/tg:
lleig, lletja, letjos/lleigs, lletges (ugly)
u → v:
blau, blava, blaus, blaves (blue)

l → l·l:
nul, nul·la, nuls, nul·les (null)
e → a:
negre, negra, negres, negres (black)

with an added *n*:
sa, sana, sans, sanes (healthy)

leg → log/logu:
homòleg, homòloga, homòlegs, homòlogues (official, approved)

s → ss:
escàs, escassa, escassos, escasses (scarce)

The following adjectives only have two forms, i.e. singular and plural, (i.e. they do not change with gender) and simply add an *s* to form the plural:

those that end in –ble, e.g.: *amable (kind)*, *noble*

those that end in –al, -el, -il, e.g.: *igual (equal)*, *fidel (faithful)*, *difícil (difficult)*

those that end in –ar, -or, e.g.: *escolar(school)*, *anterior (previous)*

those that end in –an, –ant, –ent, e.g.: *gran, elegant, prudent*

those that end in –e, e.g.: *lliure* (free), *jove* (young)

Those that end with –a in the singular, will end with –es in the plural:
hipòcrita → hipòcrites (hypocritical)
persa → perses (Persian)

The following adjectives are irregular:

mal, mala, mals, males (bad)
paral·lel, paral·lela, paral·lels, paral·leles (parallel)
tranquil, tranquil·la, tranquils, tranquil·les (calm)
car, cara, cars, cares (expensive)
rar, rara, rars, rares (rare/strange)
sant, santa, sants, santes (holy)
atent, atenta, atents, atentes (attentive)
apte, apta, aptes, aptes (apt)

Adjectives that end with –aç, -iç, -oç only have one singular form, but two plural forms that end with –os and –es in their masculine and feminine plural forms respectively:

audaç
capaç
rapaç
feliç
atroç
precoç

Descriure la gent i les coses
(describing people and things)

Com és ell? - What's he like?
Ell és simpàtic. - He's nice.

Com és ella? - What's she like?
Ella és simpàtica. - She's nice.

Com són ells? - What are they like?-m.
Ells són divertits. - They're fun. – m.

Com són elles? - What are they like?-f.
Elles són divertides. - They're fun.- f.

Ets molt seriós! – You're very serious! (m.)
Sí, però sóc divertit també! – Yes, but I'm fun, too! (m.)

Ets molt seriosa! – You're very serious! (f.)

Sí, però sóc divertida també! – Yes, but I'm fun, too! (f.)

Com sou? – What are you all like?
Som tímids. – We're shy. – m.

alt - tall
baix - short

prim - thin
gros - fat

petit/menut – small, little
gran – big, large

bonic – pretty, attractive
bell/bonic/formós - beautiful
lleig – ugly

ros(sa) – blond(e)
castany – brown-haired
pèl-roig – red-haired (m.)
pèl-roja – red-haired (f.)

interessant – interesting
divertit – fun
avorrit - boring
graciós - funny
seriós – serious

fort – strong
feble – weak

llarg - long
curt – short

bo(n) - good
dolent - bad

treballador – hardworking
mandrós – lazy

casat - married
divorciat - divorced

fàcil – easy
difícil – difficult

Com et sents? – How do you feel?
Com estàs? – How are you?

jo **em sento** – I feel
tu **et sents** – you feel
ell/ella **es sent** – he/she feels
nosaltres **ens sentim** – we feel
vosaltres **us sentiu** – you all feel
ells/elles **es senten** – they feel
jo **estic** – I am
tu **estàs** – you are
ell/ella **està** – he/she is
nosaltres **estem** – we are
vosaltres **esteu** – you all are
ells/elles **estan** – they are

bé - well
mal/malament – bad/not well

feliç/content - happy/content
trist – sad

nerviós – nervous
tranquil – calm

emocionat - excited
deprimit – depressed

cansat – tired
malalt – sick, ill

enutjat/enfadat - angry
alterat/molest/trastornat – upset
ocupat – busy
preocupat - worried

Forming the Plural

1. The general rule is to add an s to the singular:

fill→fills (sons/children)
llibre→llibres (books)
rei→reis (kings)

2. Nouns that end with an unaccented *a* end with *-es*:

dia→dies (days)
idioma→idiomes (languages)
paraula→paurales (words)

c→qu
boca→boques (mouths)
roca→roques (rocks)
tomaca→tomaques (tomatoes)

g→gu
botiga→botigues (stores/shops)
figa→figues (figs)

j→g
esponja→esponges (sponges)
taronja→taronges (oranges)

ç→c
plaça→places (town squares)

qu→qü
pasqua→pasqües (Easters)

gu→gü
aigua→aigües (waters)
llengua→llengües (tongues)

tj→tg
platja→platges (beaches)

3. Nouns that end with an accent vowel add -ns:

català→*catalans* (Catalans/Catalonians)
mà→*mans* (hands)
camí→*camins* (ways/roads)
lliçó→*lliçons* (lessons)
presentació→*presentacions* (introductions)
valencià→*valencians* (Valencians)

Exceptions:

bebé→bebés (babies)
bisturí→bisturís (scalpels)
cafè→cafés (coffees/cafés)
colibrí→colibrís (humming birds)
comité→comités (committees)
esquí→esquís (skis)
hindú→hindús (Hindus/Indians)
mamá→mamás /(moms/mums)
menú→menús (menus)
papà→papàs (dads)
paté→patés (patés)
puré→purés (purés)
sofà→sofàs (sofas)
tabú→tabús (taboos)
xampú→xampús (shampoos)

Note: The singular forms of the nouns *pantalons* and *orangutans* are *pantalon* and *orangutan*.

4. Nouns that end with an accented vowel followed by an s form the plural by adding *-os*:

anglés→anglesos (Englishmen)
avís→avisos (notices/warnings)

and with many of these, the *s* is doubled:

accés→accessos (accesses)
arròs→arrossos (rices)
cas→cassos (cases)
congrés→congressos (conferences/congresses)
gos→gossos (dogs)
interés→interessos (interests)
nas→nassos (noses)
pas→passos (steps)
pastís→pastissos (pastries)
tros→trossos (pieces)

5. Nouns that end with *ç, x, -ix* and *-tx* form the plural by adding *-os*:

braç→braços (arms)
lluç→lluços (hakes/hake fish)
calaix→calaixos (drawers/tills)
crucifix→crucifixos (crucifixes)
debuix→debuixos (drawings)
peix→peixos (fish)
capritx→capritxos (whims)
cartutx→cartutxos (cartridges)
despatx→despatxos (offices)

There are some that end with *ç* or *x* that only add an *s*:
calç→calçs (limestones)
fax→faxs (faxes)
índex→índexs (indices)

6. Nouns that end with *-sc, -st, -xt, -g* and *-ig* can form the plural with *-s* or *-os*:

bosc→boscs/boscos (forests)
casc→cascs/cascos (helmets)
gust→gusts/gustos (tastes)
text→texts/textos (texts)
desig→desigs/desitjos (desires)
passeig→passeigs/passejos (walks/strolls)

7. Masculine nouns that end with a consonant follwed by an s form the plural by adding *-os*:

curs→cursos (courses)
vals→valsos (walses)

Exceptions:

The days of the week that end in s don't add anything:

el dilluns→els dilluns (Mondays)

The following masculine nouns also add nothing:

algeps (plaster/cast)
ens (entity)
fons (bottom/back/background)
plus (plus)
socors (help)
temps (time/weather)

8. The following nouns of both genders that end with *s* also add nothing:

el cactus→els cactus (cacti/cactuses)
el llapis→els llapis (pencils)

la càries→les càries (cavities)
la pols→les pols (dusts)

9. The following nouns are used only in the plural:

els afores (suburbs/outskirts)
les alicates (pliers)
les postres (dessert)
les tisores (scissors)
les cosquerelles/pessigolles (tickles)

Al poble/A la ciutat
(around town in the Valencian Community)

These are words and phrases that I've seen walking around town and going to work on the metro in the Valencian Community where I have lived for the last several years. I hope you find them helpful. Keep in mind that this would be very similar to what you might see in parts of Catalonia since the Valencian language is almost identical to Catalan (some linguists consider Valencian to be a dialect of Catalan).

les botigues (stores/shops)
obert – open
tancat/tancada – closed
prohibit fumar – no smoking
horari – schedule (hours of operation)
Aquest (Este) establiment té fulls de reclamació. – This establishment has complaint forms. (as required by Spanish law)

les portes (doors)
empenyeu – push
estireu/tireu – pull

agafar un taxi (catching a cab)
lliure – free (available)
ocupat – busy (not available)

<u>passejant (walking around)</u>
prohibit gossos solts – prohibited dogs without leash

recipient per a reciclar – recycling bin
per a llaunes/per a llandes – for cans/tins
per als envasos – for recyclable containers
per al vidre – for glass
per a paper i cartó – for paper and cardboard
només fem – only basic trash/rubbish (not recyclable)
fems* orgànics – organic waste/trash

*escombraries in Catalan

<u>en el metro – on the subway/underground</u>

no es pot – one may not
(*no se puede* in Spanish)

No es pot viatjar amb animals a excepció dels gossos pigall.

One may not travel with animals except dogs for the blind.

pujar – to get on
baixar – to get off
abstindre – to abstain (refrain) from

Abstindre's de pujar al tren o baixar del tren després de sonar el senyal acústic de tancament de les portes.
Refrain from getting on or off the train after the closing of doors signal sounds.

No entre ni isca del tren quan senta el senyal acústic.
Don't enter or exit the train when you hear the audible signal.

Seients reservats – reserved seats

deixar – to let, allow
eixir – to leave, exit (VA)
sortir – to leave exit (CA)

Deixeu eixir* – You will see this on the doors of the train or subway car. It indicates that those waiting to to board should stand back and allow those getting off the train to do so before trying to board.

només - only

Passeu només si el tren està parat. – Only go past (this line) if the train is stopped.

tirar/estirar – pull

En cas d'emergència, tireu de la palanca de l'aparell d'alarma.
In case of emergency, pull the lever of the alarm device.

Atenció al buit entre el tren i l'andana! – Pay attention to the gap (space) between the train and the platform. (Mind the gap! in UK).

conduint (driving)
Vosté no té la prioritat. – Yield right of way. (lit. You don't have the right of way.)

Made in the USA
Middletown, DE
08 April 2020